I0492306

How to Start, Run &
Grow a Successful

# Liquor Store
# Business

## A Million Dollar Startup Guide to
## Success

By

## Jack Tillman

Published by:

## Streets of Dream Press

**Streets of Dream Press**

Cover & Interior designed

By

Jackie Bretford

*First Edition*

# CONTENTS

# INTRODUCTION

So, you want to start your own liquor store business.

Famed businessman Warren Buffett once said that when it comes to business, the view in your rearview mirror will always be much brighter than the view in your windshield.

Do you know what you are in for when you start down this road?

As I will go into further detail in this book, a liquor store business is part of a neighborhood business infrastructure. Every neighborhood has a local liquor store. No, strike that, every neighborhood has multiple liquor store businesses. Every neighborhood has basic needs that a neighborhood business supplies.

You can supply that need as the owner of a liquor store or multiple liquor stores. Neighborhoods have people, organizations, and businesses that will always need convenience items, drinks, beer, wine, and liquor for various events, functions, and parties. People will always need cigarettes, beer, tobacco or wine for one reason or another.

However, nothing is ever that easy. Not in life and especially not in business.

To own and operate your own liquor store business, you have to have some basic common sense and understanding of how business works. You have to show that you know exactly what you are doing in business if you hope to convince a financial lender or investor to part with their money.

You have to buy or lease space to operate your liquor store. You have to apply for a liquor license to legally sell alcohol to adults in the state where you operate your liquor store business. Yes, just as you would with a vehicle, you will need to keep your records in good order and renew your liquor license regularly to operate your business.

There are multiple kinds of licenses, and the one that you must apply for will depend on your business and the state that you live in. You will have to pay premiums for several kinds of insurance products, as per the circumstances of your situation, including liquor liability insurance.

You might have hundreds, or thousands or tens of thousands of individual liquor, wine and beer bottles in your inventory, along with various other merchandise like cigarettes, tobacco, candy, snacks, soda and many other items. Today's liquor store is very different from what it was 30 years ago. Now, almost every liquor store is a mini convenience store that carries a wide variety of everyday necessities, not just alcohol. You will be responsible for every one of them.

Do you know how many bottles are broken in transport, accidentally or by clumsy customers, every day, week, month and year in a liquor store business?

I am not trying to discourage you. I want you to understand that owning and operating a liquor store business is a serious undertaking. You bought this book for a reason, and I want to encourage and enhance those reasons.

As with any business, you will need discipline and determination to succeed. A lot of people think that just starting a business is when all of the hard work ends. However, starting a business is when the hard work really begins. There will always be some work to do when you own a business. The work never ends when you own a business, especially a liquor store business.

This book will help you start your first liquor store business. However, if you are successful and want to generate higher profits, you may want to open more than one liquor store. If you own more than one liquor store business, that means you will have to contend with more bookkeeping, accounting and even more inventory to deal with. Imagine being solely responsible for tens of thousands of individual bottles of liquor, wine, and beer. If you open multiple liquor store business locations, you will be. That is a lot of responsibility that cannot be taken lightly.

In this book, I will give you as much information as possible to help you start your liquor store business. Treat this book as a template for what you need to do to become a business owner. The circumstances and details of your personal life and how you managed to start your liquor store business are distinct. I will give you the tools you need, but you will have to use them as you see fit, given your personal circumstances.

You bought this book for a reason. There must be a drive, a dream or some passionate ambition that is leading you in such a direction. Just remember, if your head is in the clouds, keep your feet firmly on the ground. Be realistic about your ambitions and what you need to do to achieve them. Nothing in life is easy.

Some people just like being called businesspeople. It takes a lot of blood, sweat, and tears, and incalculable amounts of work, to become a successful businessperson, especially in the liquor store business.

So, you want to be a liquor store owner?

Let's get started...

# WHY A LIQUOR STORE

There are certain absolute truths in life when it comes to taking potential advantage of readily available business opportunities. There is always a way to make a dollar if you do the hard work, do your research, understand the market and put your mind to it.

People will always need to pay their taxes. People will always need a place to live, or, more specifically, a dwelling, to pay rent or a mortgage and live their personal lives. People will always need to eat.

One of the most essential absolute truths in life, however, depending on whom you ask, is that certain people will always enjoy their daily beer, liquor, wine, cigarettes, tobacco or many other similar habits. During the good times, and indeed, during the bad times, people will always drink alcohol and will have a need for a smoke.

In fact, some would say the only business that could withstand a recession is the liquor store. While you should not predicate opening a liquor store business solely on such an idea, as running a business is a highly complex endeavor, there is some smattering of truth to such a statement.

There will always be a market for alcohol and tobacco. Even though the general widespread use of alcoholic beverages is prone to unpredictable fluctuation, people never stop drinking alcohol altogether. Like most products, demand for alcohol can go up and down. People may drink alcohol more than others, but people will always drink alcohol.

However, the fact that people need, want or find reasons to drink alcohol should not be your main reason for opening a liquor store business. As a businessperson, you should have a lot more than one reason. The reasons will vary depending on where you plan to open your liquor store. You shouldn't have just one reason for opening a liquor store business.

The success of a liquor store business is mainly predicated on its location and proximity to its consumer demographic, like all businesses. Not to mention, a liquor store not only carries alcohol but hundreds of other everyday need items like cigarettes, candy, gum, chips, juice, soda and even bottles of water.

You should be very realistic about how the liquor store business works. There is a myriad of federal, state and municipal level regulations that you will have to learn about and contend with. You must understand that it takes significant investment capital to start a liquor business. Like most things, it takes money to make money. Exactly where your liquor store business is located, the local and federal laws governing its operations and the saturation of already existing liquor businesses in the market will also dictate the success of your liquor store business.

In short, you may need to use your initial liquor store business as a marketing plan for eventual expansion. Start with opening one store, but understand that you may eventually need to open more to generate healthy profits.

As you will learn, most neighborhoods need more than one liquor store to meet their demand.

Exhaustively research your neighborhood and customer demographics. Know what they want, what they drink and what they want to drink. You have to give people what they want when it comes to alcohol, or you won't be in the liquor store business for very long.

You will learn about all of these subjects, and more, in this book. When you develop a baseline introduction to the intricacies of owning a liquor store business, then, and only then, could you have success running one.

It is not my intention to make such a business endeavor sound half as easy as it may seem right now. Running a liquor store is not easy. However, with sufficient investing capital, planning, and operational foresight, it is indeed doable. It can even be profitable if you know what you are doing, understand the market and take your bookkeeping and accounting extremely seriously.

So, the question remains, as referenced in this very chapter title: why a liquor store?

Let's answer that question before we start talking about how to start a liquor store business.

# THREE BIG REASONS TO OPEN A LIQUOR STORE

## A VITAL PART OF NEIGHBORHOOD BUSINESS INFRASTRUCTURE

Businesses and the neighborhoods that they operate in are inextricably linked. They are linked almost symbiotically. One cannot prosper or survive without the other. Neighborhoods and neighborhood-centric businesses both vitally need each other to survive.

Every neighborhood has a vital business infrastructure that benefits the neighborhood and its connected businesses.

In almost every neighborhood in the United States, there is a predictable staple of businesses operating there. Neighborhood businesses. Think about it.

The neighborhood laundromat. The neighborhood supermarket or corner store. The neighborhood insurance office. The neighborhood restaurant. The neighborhood hotel. The neighborhood dental office. The neighborhood carwash. The neighborhood auto mechanic shop.

Each of these businesses, and more, can be found in almost every American neighborhood. Such companies offer services that nearly every American neighborhood needs. Such businesses can only thrive, prosper, and profit if they provide services that benefit the neighborhoods from which they operate.

What is missing from the list of neighborhood-centric businesses that usually comprise a basic neighborhood business infrastructure?

The neighborhood liquor store.

In fact, most neighborhoods have multiple liquor stores within their boundaries, especially in big cities. Such businesses are multiple-competitor businesses or expansion stores owned by a single person or business entity.

Neighborhoods go through good and bad times. People move in and out of neighborhoods. Yet, people will always need and want to drink alcohol. During the good times and during the bad times.

Even though the demand for alcohol will invariably go up and down, someone or some business will always open a liquor store. Like most other neighborhood-centric businesses, neighborhoods will always have liquor stores operating within their boundaries. Liquor stores will always need neighborhoods to exist in and operate from. There will always be a neighborhood liquor store business, multiples of them, operating within the boundaries of a neighborhood.

If you have the investment capital, have done the necessary customer demographic research and profit projections, and are realistic about your business operations goals, then why not *you*? A liquor store business, like many other businesses, is a vital part of a neighborhood's business infrastructure. You are reading this book for a reason.

If not you, it will be someone else who opens a neighborhood liquor store business. If you have the drive, why not do it?

## NEIGHBORHOOD FUNCTIONS, EVENTS, AND PARTIES WILL ALWAYS REQUIRE AN ALCOHOL SUPPLIER

Why are the previous neighborhood businesses such a vital part of a neighborhood's infrastructure? Why is such neighborhood-centric business inextricably connected to the neighborhoods that they do business in and operate from?

Most people who live in neighborhoods own cars. So, local car washes and auto mechanics will always have neighborhood business as long as the neighborhood exists.

Most people who live in neighborhoods eat breakfast, lunch, and dinner and need to buy food and groceries. So, the local supermarket will always have neighborhood business from people in the neighborhood.

By now, you must see exactly where I am going with this connective theme and train of thought.

Families, local businesses, legal-drinking-age college students, union workers, construction workers, office workers, police departments, and every kind of neighborhood inhabitant, business, and organization will need alcohol for their functions, parties, and events.

Or will need and want alcohol for the sake of having alcohol.

People who live and work in neighborhoods have birthday parties, retirement parties, anniversary parties, picnics, BBQs, dance parties, social mixers, wine-and-cheese mixers, privately catered events, and many more kinds of events all year long.

People who live and work in neighborhoods will always need a reliable go-to source for their specific events, functions, and party related alcohol needs.

Buying, owning and operating a neighborhood liquor store business is no easy feat, as we will discuss in later chapters. Just consider that whoever owns the local liquor store is the main go-to for all the neighborhood's alcohol needs. That is a lot of responsibility and requires significant internal bookkeeping and accounting, especially if the business is brisk.

People who drink alcohol have specific tastes, specific brands that they are habitually loyal to and brands that they want to try or acquire for friends or party needs. Some people walk into a liquor store and don't know what they want, but they want help buying something unique or a brand name.

Supermarkets and corner stores carry only a limited selection of liquor, wine, spirits, and beer. It is the local liquor store that locals depend on to take a wide selection of alcohol for their functions, parties, and event needs.

In every neighborhood, there will always be a function, party, event, or private event that requires large amounts of alcohol. When you choose a neighborhood locale to open your liquor store, you will become the primary go-to source for all of that neighborhood's alcohol needs throughout the year. Think about that.

## MOST NEIGHBORHOODS REQUIRE MORE THAN ONE LIQUOR STORE

According to a July 2016 census, New York City has over 8.5 million inhabitants.[1] As of May 2017, it was estimated that about 4,000,000 people lived in Los Angeles, California.[2] Projections calculated by Texas state authorities estimated that about 7,000,000 people were living in the city of Houston.[3]

Think about the sheer number of neighborhood insurance offices, dental offices, car washes, auto mechanic shops and supermarkets that are needed to service and accommodate all of the people who live in and inhabitant the previously mentioned cities? How many car wash business establishments do you think are needed to accommodate all of the people who drive cars in New York City? Do you think there is only *one* supermarket operating within the boundaries of New York City?

Picking a prime location is vital when opening a liquor store. It is all about location, location, location, as the old saying goes. You need to research where you may open a liquor store, the population who live there and why they would patronize your liquor store business, subjects I will expand on in later chapters.

You also have to consider current liquor market saturation and be aware of how many other liquor stores are in the area. Open a liquor store business with some healthy strategic distance from other liquor store businesses. Otherwise, it will be hard to profit. Each business will lower prices to undercut the other, and no one will prosper.

The point is, if you look hard enough, you will almost always find a prime location to start your liquor store business. You can find a suitable business location to serve a population demographic that is not being served, or is only partially served, by nearby liquor stores. It won't be easy, but it will be doable.

Most cities and neighborhoods need more than one supermarket, laundromat, or auto mechanic shop to adequately serve their inhabitants.

There isn't just one liquor store business in New York City, Los Angeles or Houston. Wherever you live, and unless you live in a very small town or hamlet with a small population, you are supplying a need and servicing a demand if you open a neighborhood liquor store business in a moderate to large-sized city.

In very large metropolitan cities in the United States, it is not unheard of for multiple liquor stores to operate within a one- to five-mile radius.

According to companies that conduct such business-related research, over 37,600 liquor stores were operating in the United States in 2017. In 2015, there were an estimated 36,700 such businesses in operation. That number should reach 38,700 by 2018 and grow to over 40,000 by the year 2019.

Starting a liquor store business is very expensive. As I will discuss in the next chapter, obtaining a liquor license can be a moderate to very expensive endeavor. It is also quite a bureaucratic headache to acquire a liquor license. The liquor store business is heavily regulated by your state's Alcoholic Beverage Control board and the Bureau of Alcohol, Tobacco, and Firearms. There will be a lot of regulatory oversight you will have to contend with when you start a liquor store business.

Yet, as you can see by the data presented in the chart above, the number of viable liquor store establishments increases by a few hundred to over a thousand every year. The number of liquor store openings has increased steadily since 2015 and is projected to keep increasing, if only incrementally.

Neighborhoods grow and decrease in population all the time. Economies thrive and recede in cycles. Yet, people still need and want to drink. If you live in a city with a population of over half a million people, never mind 8,000,000, there will always be a need for multiple liquor stores to operate.

Someone with drive, attention to detail, and a realistic grasp of the business market is going to open a liquor store. As I have asked before: why not you?

1 "Current Estimates for New York City's Population for July 2016." http://www1.nyc.gov/site/planning/data-maps/nyc-population/current-future-populations.page

2 Grad, Shelby. *"Los Angeles hits a milestone: 4 million people and counting."* The Los Angeles Times. May 2, 2017.

3 "Texas Population Projections, 2017." https://www.dshs.texas.gov/chs/popdat/ST2017.shtm

4 "Beer & Wine & Liquor Stores Industry (Naiks 44531)." United States Beer & Wine & Liquor Stores Industry Report, Jan. 2018, pp. 14-196

# Estimated Cost

Opening a liquor store requires dealing with various government agencies to obtain licenses and permits. Just like any other business, if you follow the steps correctly, you can get it done in a reasonable amount of time. Opening a liquor store successfully depends significantly on your access to investment capital, or money. It takes money to make money, and you are going to need a lot of money to open a liquor store. Considering whether you qualify for a business loan should be an option you seriously consider if you can.

There is no one-size-fits-all calculation that can estimate how much it will cost you to open a liquor store business. However, how much you will ultimately pay to open a liquor store depends upon a number of factors that rely heavily on where you live, exactly where you plan to open your liquor store business, what kind of alcohol you sell, and how and when you intend to sell it.

The costs associated with starting a liquor store vary from state to state, city to city and county to county. It really depends on where you live, how big you want your liquor store business to be and the rules of the liquor regulating authorities in your state. It also depends on how many people live in the neighborhood and on your customer demographic, where you plan to open your liquor store.

The point is that this book can only give you a general guideline for starting a liquor store business. The specifics and particulars concerning exactly how much money *you* will require to open a liquor store business will vary.

If you live in a moderate-sized, non-metropolitan city, it might cost you $25,000 to $50,000 to open a liquor store business. However, if you live in a large metropolitan city with a large population and substantial potential customer traffic, you might have to pay anywhere from $250,000 to $ 1 million to open a liquor store successfully.

Paying more than a million dollars is even potentially possible, depending on the situation.

Paying for the store purchase and for the liquor license are two separate issues. The Alcoholic Beverage Control Board awards liquor licenses in your state. A liquor license allows you to sell alcohol to adults and must be renewed anywhere from one to three years, depending on where your liquor store business operates. The expense of a liquor license can vary wildly depending on your location as well. A liquor license in California can cost upwards of $400,000.[5]

## ESTIMATED COST OF OPENING A LIQUOR STORE IN A SMALL TO MID-SIZE CITY

| ITEMS | COST |
|---|---|
| Lease Deposit, Insurance & License Fees | $3,500 - $5,000 |
| Build out/Layout | $2,500 - $25,000 |
| Equipment (Walk-in Cooler, Etc.) | $10,000 - $35,000 |
| Counter Top & Shelving | $3,000 - $15,000 |

| | |
|---|---|
| Lighting & Signage | $2,000 - $5,000 |
| POS, Credit Card & Video Equipment | $5,000 - $7,500 |
| Inventory | $15,000-$50,000 |
| Employee Training & Uniform | $1,500 |
| Startup Cash | $5,000 |
| **TOTAL:** | **$47,500 - $149,000** |

The listing price for a liquor store business in Fresno, California, can run about $135,000. In Hammonton, New Jersey, which has a high population density, is near major highways and is a location that can generate a lot of traffic, a liquor business was recently listed for $2,700 000.[6]

The point is that if your potential store is located near a high-traffic area, like a highway where people are very likely to stop by you will have to pay more to purchase your store and liquor license.

You can buy a liquor license from someone who already owns one and who is looking to sell their business and license. Still, such a transaction would have to be conducted in coordination with the Alcoholic Beverage

Control board in your state. You can save a lot of money this way, but you should know it's far from a guaranteed solution.

You should also be aware that the liquor store business is heavily regulated, as mentioned before, and that only a finite number of liquor licenses are sold to business owners each year, from state to state, city to city, and county to county.

## U.S. STATES – ESTIMATED NUMBER OF ESTABLISHMENTS
### YEAR: 2018

| Area Name | Employee Size of Establishment | | | | | | | | Total Establishments |
|---|---|---|---|---|---|---|---|---|---|
|  | 1-4 Emps. | 5-9 Emps. | 10-19 Emps. | 20-49 Emps. | 50-99 Emps. | 100-249 Emps. | 250-499 Emps. | >500 Emps. |  |
| Pennsylvania | 1,082 | 634 | 183 | 22 | 0 | 0 | 0 | 0 | 2,100 |
| Rhode Island | 132 | 68 | 38 | 5 | 0 | 0 | 0 | 0 | 265 |
| South Carolina | 350 | 147 | 83 | 16 | 1 | 0 | 0 | 0 | 265 |
| South Dakota | 32 | 34 | 13 | 1 | 0 | 0 | 0 | 0 | 469 |
| Tennessee | 367 | 224 | 65 | 4 | 0 | 0 | 0 | 0 | 87 |
| Texas | 1,333 | 426 | 150 | 55 | 17 | 9 | 0 | 0 | 2,148 |
| Utah | 116 | 82 | 22 | 5 | 1 | 0 | 0 | 0 | 266 |
| Vermont | 150 | 286 | 45 | 6 | 1 | 1 | 0 | 0 | 40 |
| Virginia | 105 | 156 | 48 | 8 | 2 | 0 | 0 | 0 | 533 |
| Washington | 191 | 125 | 86 | 24 | 6 | 9 | 0 | 0 | 777 |
| West Virginia | 271 | 109 | 41 | 7 | 0 | 0 | 0 | 0 | 496 |
| Wisconsin | 95 | 35 | 22 | 7 | 0 | 0 | 0 | 0 | 318 |
| Wyoming | 28 | 38 | 27 | 0 | 0 | 0 | 0 | 0 | 175 |

**(Source: Barnes Report)**

It has been estimated that there will be about 2,100 liquor stores in Pennsylvania and 2,148 in Texas. In Utah, a very religiously conservative and Mormon state, there will be only an estimated 67 official liquor stores. In the state of Wisconsin, there will be only 70 liquor stores. I am showing you these figures because this information will go a long way toward helping you determine how much money you need to open your liquor store.

The number of liquor stores, or businesses allowed to sell liquor in restaurants, clubs, and bars, is relatively small in Utah compared to other states. Buying a liquor store in Utah could cost you tens of thousands to hundreds of thousands of dollars, depending on the location.

Just acquiring liquor liability insurance certification coverage can cost you anywhere from $1,000 to $4,000. Consider that this is in a religiously conservative state with strict zoning laws. The estimates for starting a liquor store in Pennsylvania and Texas are bound to be much higher, since the fact that so many establishments already exist indicates that there is a population that demands such a supply.

You should also find out what applications and permits you may need from the Alcohol and Tobacco Trade and Tax Bureau, which regulates the national selling, production, and importation of alcoholic products. It will cost money to apply for any permits from this authority, but it will cost a lot more if you don't and then realize you need them.

It is not my intention to discourage you from business ownership ambitions. I only wish to point out that there are many factors you should consider before starting a liquor store. People will always drink beer, but the alcohol business can be unpredictable. The main factor you should consider when estimating start-up costs is location, location, location.

For fundamental estimation, you should be prepared to pay anywhere from $50,000 to $250,000 to start up your first liquor store business. Be aware that these basic estimates may be only initial start-up costs to get your business off the ground and operational.

Starting a liquor store business is going to cost you some money, no doubt. However, trying to start a liquor store business while being woefully unprepared and without your paperwork is going to cost you a whole lot more money in the short and long term.

I highly recommend that you secure legal advice from a good attorney as you endeavor to start a liquor store. There is just too much paperwork, bureaucracy, regulations, and rules involved for you to do it all on your own.

www.parkcity.org/how-do-i/business-licenses/alcohol-liquor-license

5 "How Much Does a Liquor License Cost in California?" http://licenselocators.com/how-much-does-a-liquor-license-cost/

6 "Capital Needed To Start a Liquor Store." http://smallbusiness.chron.com/capital-needed-start-liquor-store-10356.html

# 8 STEPS TO OPENING YOUR OWN LIQUOR STORE

OK, now you are ready to take the first steps toward opening your own liquor store. I highly recommend that, along with the counsel of a professional lawyer, you enlist the aid of a liquor, wine and beer industry consultant. This is someone who knows the industry, how the business works and who can guide you in your decision-making. You could also enlist the advice and counsel of a liquor store owner who is already in the business. If you are adamant about opening a liquor store, consider information as currency. The more you have, the better off you will be.

Based on my own experiences, I have devised an 8-step process that you can follow, or adapt as you see fit to your own circumstances, to help you as you open your own liquor store business.

1. Budget and Finance

2. Business Plan

3. Site selection

4. Uncle Sam (Licensing & Permits)

5. Build out/Layout

6. Merchandising

7. Pricing and POS

8. Grand Opening

# BUDGET AND FINANCE

There are many economic factors you must consider when opening a startup. Economic factors that you must consider when starting a liquor store business include, but are in no way limited to:

- Rent or lease payments
- Employee payroll
- Utility bill payments
- State, city and local liquor license fees
- Liquor license processing fees
- Merchandising and inventory purchasing
- Legal counsel and retention
- Liquor liability insurance
- Zoning law restrictions
- Vendors to Buy from
- Music license (if you plan to play copyrighted music on public speakers in a place of business)

Do you have the economic means to pay a monthly rent or lease payment for a place of business? It's a serious matter not to be taken lightly. The monthly rent for a liquor store can cost you anywhere from several thousand to tens of thousands of dollars a month. Depending on your rental or lease agreement, such payments may be subject to unannounced increases as well.

For estimation's sake, the price to lease a small storefront in New Jersey or New York can cost you $70,000 to $85,000. But on the other hand, leasing a 1200-1500 SQF storefront in cities like Memphis, TN, or Louisville, KY may only cost you $3,000 to $4,000.

Do you plan to have any employees? When you are running a liquor store business, you have to keep track of inventory, how much money you are spending, how much revenue you are generating to pay expenses and keep track of profits. There is a lot of work and meticulous bookkeeping involved with liquor store ownership. Hiring one or more employees, part-time or full-time, at minimum wage will cost you tens of thousands of dollars per person annually.

How much you pay in utility payments for a liquor store business will depend on where you open your business and how many hours a day you plan to stay open for operations. Count on it from being hundreds to thousands of dollars per month, if not more. You will have to apply for a liquor license or authorization to sell liquor in a place of business from your state's Alcoholic Beverage Control board.

As previously mentioned, that can cost anywhere from a few hundred dollars to a few thousand dollars, depending on where you live. It can take you anywhere from six months to a year to acquire your liquor license.

Alcoholic beverage control boards do not just hand them out, and they are notoriously hard to get. Also know that after you get your liquor license on the state level, you may have to get one at the city and local level as well, but again, that will depend on where you live. Processing fees for liquor licenses usually start at $100, but can cost you more.

Merchandising and stocking your inventory is going to cost you money, especially if you plan to open a mid- to large-sized store with a wide variety of alcohol for sale. Merchandising is everything you do as a businessperson to promote and sell a trademarked business brand in your place of business.

You may not be able to just sell Absolut vodka or Johnnie Walker Scotch whiskey without getting legal permission from agents and distributors of the companies that sell those brands. Once you do, you can get advertising placards and signs to sell such products in your store. (We will go into merchandising much deeper in a subsequent chapter.)

Along with merchandising, you have to stock your shelves with liquor to sell. This is your inventory. You have to continuously monitor your inventory to see what is selling, what isn't, and adjust prices accordingly.

Depending on the size of your store and the location that you open it, you could spend anywhere from $15,000 to $50,000, or more, on your inventory. Do the research and find out what your potential consumer demographic wants to drink. Learn what sells quickly and stock up on it in your first few months. Having full inventories and well-stocked shelves for prolonged periods of time will not bring you profits.

Zoning laws are legal restrictions that can severely restrict exactly where and at what times you can sell liquor to the general public. Some strict state, city, and local ordinances prohibit the sale of alcohol near schools, churches, on Sundays, or at certain times of day. Or they will allow it just as long as you pay more money for the privilege, while running your establishment responsibly and never selling to minors. Zoning laws vary widely from state to state, city to city, and county to county across the country.

As previously mentioned, you would do well to look into applying for a small-business loan, business credit, or a personal loan to help you start a liquor store. The initial costs for opening your liquor store may just cover the costs of opening it. Once your store is operational and running, you may need to hire additional employees, expand your inventory, pay rent increases, pay for repairs, etc.

There will be many unforeseen costs associated with running a business, in addition to the usual costs. If you do apply for financing or a loan, try not to use more than 10% to 15% of your own money in such an endeavor. Also, realize that if you do qualify for such a business loan, you may be liable for paying up to 20% on a down payment.

This is only a sample of all the economic and documentation considerations that you will have to make when opening your liquor store business. This is by no means an exhaustive list. The factors that you will have to consider in starting your liquor store business will be unique to you, as they would be to every other potential businessperson.

But if you are thinking about finding money from other sources, here are some great ideas.

1. Your own savings/401K, etc.
2. Home equity line of credit (this is how I got started with mine)
3. Family funding (where your parents, siblings help you with a personal loan)
4. Create a partnership with people who have the money
5. Crowdfunding
6. Applying for a small business loan at your local bank

Sit down, take a piece of paper, try to analyze each and every option and then see which one seems more doable for you. You can even do a mix-and-match here. For example, you need $100,000 to open your liquor store, but you only have $50,000. One idea is to ask one or two like-minded friends or family to come in as 50% partners, with you holding 50% and the other two getting 25% each.

As for crowdfunding, I have never done it, but I have seen people do it. You can make a list of 10-20 people that you know. Ask each of them to invest $10,000 for a 7% stake in your company. If 10 of them agree, you will have

$100,000 and have only paid out 70% of your business. The remaining 30% is still yours for FREE.

You just have to be creative, remember that when there is strong willpower to achieve something, there is always a way to get there.

Applying for a loan at the bank is the hardest of all other methods I outlined above. In the event you have no other option but to apply for a loan, you do have to do some research first.

First, make a list of banks you want to apply to. It is not a good idea to apply to multiple banks at once; instead, compile a list of, say, 4 banks. Visit them and talk in depth with their business loan department to find out whether that bank offers loans for your type of projects. Some banks do not offer restaurant loans.

In my experience, I have noticed that smaller local banks are typically more inclined to offer loans to local family-owned restaurants, liquor stores, coffee shops, and other similar businesses than some of the bigger banks. But that may not be true in every part of the country, so it is best to talk to at least 3-4 banks and get a feel for whether they are really into this kind of business financing before you submit your application.

Sometimes, your local business brokers or commercial real estate agents can guide you to the right bank, as they often deal with similar situations and know which banks are more favorable to this sort of loan. You can also ask your bank, which you deal with every day, for its advice.

Once you narrow it down to two banks, visit them, meet with their loan officer, and see what their requirements are. Just remember, every bank will have similar requirements, but they can still vary widely based on factors like the down payment they require, the collateral they will need from you, and whether they offer SBA-assisted loans. Your goal would be to work with a bank that offers an SBA loan. SBA stands for the Small Business Administration. This is where the federal government guarantees part of your loan to the bank.

Most of the time, SBA offers a guarantee (typically 50-80%) to the bank on your behalf, so banks are somewhat more lenient in approving the loan, as they are not at risk for the full amount they are giving you. But the downside to this is that the amount of paperwork you have to furnish is monumental in most cases.

SBA's requirements can be extensive, so be prepared to gather a lot of paperwork.

Another drawback to an SBA loan is that it can take up to 4 months to get approval, as they move more slowly than most banks. In their defense, they do have a lot of applicants. They have to go through all of them, and it is always first-come, first-served, so be patient.

But if you have a larger down payment (30% or higher) or have some good collateral to offer, then you can opt out of SBA loans and get any bank to provide you a conventional business loan. Provided you have all your ducks in a row, like your credit is in excellent shape, your tax returns show good incomes for previous years, etc.

When you talk to any bank, they will hand you something called a loan package. Most of the time, the package will include a checklist of documents you need to furnish, along with a loan application and other waiver forms, depending on your bank.

One thing to keep in mind: all banks and commercial lenders have to follow guidelines set by federal and state banking authorities. Also, every bank will look at the LTV (Loan-to-Value) ratio of the property or business you are looking to buy. LTV is essentially the ratio of the actual value of the business you are looking to buy or lease to the amount they can loan you.

Let's look at the list of documents you will need to prepare for submission to your bank. Some of these items I will mention here may not be on your bank's checklist, but do gather them anyway, as it will make you look more professional and business-like.

### **Here is What You Need to Gather:**

1. You need to get copies of at least the last three years of personal tax returns, and make sure the copies are signed.

2. Your resume (they may not even ask you for it, but remember the person that may approve your loan may never meet you, but this way at least he or she gets to see who you are and how qualified you are.)

3. Copy of your Corp. Articles (yes, you have to get this done before you even apply for your loan. I will touch on how to file a corporation in the next chapter)

4. Personal financial statement for all Corp. Officers or members. Make sure to sign it. If you are married and file joint tax returns, your wife needs to have one prepared for her as well. You can also prepare a joint personal financial statement for both of you and make sure both of you sign it.

5. Copy of the commercial appraisal (in the event you are buying a location instead of leasing)

6. Copy of signed purchase agreement and Letter of intent (in the event you are buying)

7. Copy of your EIN (Employer's Identification Number) issued by the IRS

8. Copy of all members/partners' Driver's licenses and social security cards

9. A well-thought-out and expertly written Business Plan (not a store-bought one or copy-pasted one, one that is written for your specific business, get help if you need to,

but this has to be a well-thought-out plan, do it like your life depends on it, trust me on this.)

10. The loan application is all filled out. Use a computer and printer if possible; if not, write very clearly so it is easy to read.

11. A cover letter addressed to the loan department where you describe what is in the package and thank them for reviewing your loan application, and lastly, tell them where they can easily reach you if they need further help or other documents from you. It just makes you look more professional.

Now, remember to organize these papers with nice tabs and put them in a binder folder so anyone can open the folder, see the tabs, and go directly to the specific section.

If you are applying for an SBA-specific business loan, SBA may also provide a loan package with additional documents and forms to fill out, but they will mostly ask for the same things I just mentioned. They will have you fill out many more forms, and don't worry, you do not have to visit the SBA office separately. They work through your local banks so the loan officer you deal with will furnish you all of that.

# BUSINESS PLAN

You need a realistic business plan for opening your store, and then you should update it monthly, quarterly, or semi-annually as needed. A business plan is an operational plan that shows you know how much money you are spending on your business for expenses, how much profit you are making, how much money you are losing, how much money you need or want to make and the estimated projections of such numbers that extend outward for three or five years.

A business plan presents your business's operational health in hard data, numbers, and charts. Whether your business is prospering or failing, an exhaustively detailed, regularly updated business plan will tell you before such events occur. A good business plan will detail the operational goals you aim to achieve. A good business plan is also augmented by good bookkeeping. It will detail obstacles, such as market volatility, consumer demand cycles, and increases in rent or inventory purchase prices, and outline strategies to overcome them.

A business plan explains how you started your business, how it is doing today, and how it will be doing in three or five years. You will need a business plan, not just for yourself, but so you can always be apprised of the health of your business and keep accurate books. Having a business plan also helps if you want to secure financing, such as a business loan, from a bank or an individual private lender. Potential lenders and investors will appreciate an accurate business plan as a mark of professionalism and will consider your liquor store business low risk for lending.

Your business plan could be dozens, a hundred, or more pages long, depending on the size of your business and the scale at which you want to operate in the future.

Here are eight categories that can act as a primer for your own business plan. This is just a template for the sake of example, as your business plan will include factors, data, and financial considerations that are singular, distinct, and unique to your business situation.

Your business plan should make considerations for the following topics:

- Executive summary
- Company overview
- Industry overview
- Consumer Trends
- Overview of Competitors
- Overview of Marketing
- Operations Strategy Plan
- Financial Strategy

An executive summary is a basic introduction and overview of your overall business plan. Think of it as the coming attraction or trailer for an eventual movie. It is brief and provides brief bullet points of information. It should tell the reader what they are about the read.

Your executive summary should be a paragraph or no longer than a page. You use the executive summary to briefly describe your liquor store business, present evidence from research and market analysis that shows you are meeting an unfulfilled need for a demographic or population, and explain why your liquor store business is primed to fulfill and satisfy that need.

Although the executive summary is the first thing that potential financial lenders and investors will read, it should be the last thing that you write after you have compiled all the necessary data needed to complete your full business plan.

The company overview is part of your business plan where you thoroughly explain the founding of your liquor business and its current operational functions. Talk about how you started your business and all of the actions you undertook to launch it.

If you formed a business alliance with local businesspeople, secured beneficial financing or made a deal with a supplier that greatly helped you to launch your liquor store business, then discuss it here. Sell the reader on what it is that makes your liquor store business so uniquely qualified and market-positioned to prosper in your business plan.

In the industry overview section of your business plan, you will expound on the local market, a unique demographic niche, or business opportunities that your liquor store is primed to take advantage of and supply.

Explain exactly what kind of consumer demand your liquor store business will serve on a consistent and hopefully long-term basis. Explain whether you will stock hard-to-find liquors or microbrew craft beers, or whether you have an untapped and unserved demographic you are primed to serve. Lay out your strategy to keep your business healthy.

The consumer trends overview section of your business plan will describe your customer base or the business demographic that will patronize your liquor store business. Where exactly will your liquor store be located? Why? In what neighborhood? Who are the people and workers inhabiting your neighborhood base of operations? Are they working class? Is it a college town with numerous local colleges or universities?

Have you taken a survey or researched to find out what your consumer demographic drinks when they drink and when they want to buy their drinks? Show that you understand why your customer demographic will patronize your liquor store, and why you are confident you can always meet that need.

Use the competition overview to describe what it is that sets your liquor store business apart from your competitors. Your competition in the liquor store business falls into two categories: direct competitors and indirect competitors. Your direct competitors are other liquor stores owned by people like you that operate in your area and serve the same demographic as you.

Restaurants, bars, and clubs that serve a different alcohol-based product to your same customer demographics are indirect competitors.

Explain in your business plan why your direct and indirect competitors will pose no obstacle to the success of your own liquor store business.

Your marketing overview, or marketing plan, explains how you will promote your liquor store and how you plan to make a profit. You will need to list every alcoholic product that you will sell in your liquor store business and why you think it will sell. How much money will you charge customers for the products that you sell, and explain why, as based on the dictates of the market or consumer demand?

What is it about the physical location that will help you sell your product better? Will your liquor store business have a presence on social media? Also, what promotional plans will you use to attract new customers? You should also explain how you plan to retain your loyal customer base.

How will you meet all of your liquor store business goals? Your operations strategy plan will lay out exactly how you plan to meet your goals, make profits and stay in business for the long term. In what cost-cutting ways will you order, buy and turn over inventory? In what unique ways will you sell your products? How will you prevent shrinkage? Shrinkage is an alcohol industry and business term relating to the loss of product inventory by wholly involuntary means.

Bottles can break on delivery or due to a clumsy customer in your store. Shrinkage can also be caused by burglary and theft. What are your long-term goals? Do you plan to expand and open more than one liquor store business? How will you go about doing this? You must explain all of this and more in the operations strategy section of your business plan.

In your financial plan, you discuss your overhead, or how much you pay to keep the store operational, as well as your revenue, or the profits that are used to pay for your business expenses. You will also explain exactly what products are selling more than others and how you plan to expand on that. The final part of your financial plan should explain exactly how business profits will increase over the next three or five years.

## 5 BIGGEST MISCONCEPTIONS ABOUT BUSINESS PLAN

### *No one ever told them about a business plan before*

It's natural that many liquor shop owners may not have been exposed to the process of creating a business plan. While some businesses can succeed without one, it is not the recommended way to open a business. The first thing you may want to familiarize yourself with is the different points the business plan will highlight.

### *They are confused about where to start*

So, a business owner may know they need a business plan, but may not understand where to start, so they decide not to do it. This is not ever a good idea. Every business owner has to start somewhere. You have to start your business plan if you want to use it to bring your dreams to life.

### They think it is just too hard

Starting a business plan doesn't have to be difficult, but you have to put in the work. It also requires a great deal of thoughtfulness and time. While planning doesn't always guarantee success, not planning almost certainly leads to failure. It may not seem like fun, but losing all your money in a terrible business doesn't seem too fun either. To start your plan, you don't have to start from scratch. There are many online resources to get you started.

### They think their business is too small to be worth the trouble

You might think that a business plan would be overkill because you are just starting a small business. But even a small business would benefit from a well-crafted business plan. Even small businesses have hundreds of things to keep track of and consider.

### *You think you can keep all the plans in your head*

Sometimes, business owners think they should rely on their mental abilities or just their memories rather than taking the time to develop a business plan. But what they are not considering when starting a business is that they will be way too busy with day-to-day operations to remember everything they need to do to open their business.

# SITE SELECTION

A driving factor in the success of your liquor store business will be location, location, location. Your liquor store business must be located in a prime location to be extremely business advantageous and to make the most of the nearby customer demographic, i.e., the people in your neighborhood.

Remember, unless you are opening a liquor store to carry only expensive liquor and wine around a rich neighborhood, the best location should have the following:

- Moderate foot traffic
- Mid to low-income housing
- Median income level less than $50K/year

- Blue-collar neighborhood
- Mixed-race neighborhood

Is the location spot that you are considering for your liquor store business site already saturated with other liquor store businesses in the area? Then why would you build there? For one thing, you'll have to sell your products at much lower prices just to get into the local market, which won't help your profit margins at all, since customers will already have other stores to patronize.

Also, you will give your direct competitors every reason to pull every promotional strategy they have to try to put you out of business, since they have been in the area longer than you. You need a liquor store location that is readily accessible to your customer demographic but also strategically distant from your direct and indirect competitors, if possible.

Do you know your neighborhood? You won't sell a lot of product if you start a liquor store business in a zealot-like, religious enclave neighborhood or one with numerous anti-alcohol zoning laws. How young or old are the inhabitants of your neighborhood?

Mature people drink alcohol, but legal drinking age young people have much more disposable income at the ready. Is the neighborhood full of hard-working family types who may need a place for their alcohol needs? What do the people in your neighborhood like to drink?

You need to put your liquor store business where people can get what they want from it. Here is an added bonus idea: we all know that the new trendy thing is smoke hookahs, right? Why not set up a section in your store to sell various hookahs and the accessories that go with them?

There are numerous, strict anti-alcohol zoning laws that vary from state to state, city to city, and county to county. Zoning laws can restrict when you can sell alcohol.

Zoning laws can prevent you from selling alcohol on a Sunday, near schools or religious institutions. Or you may have to pay extra for your liquor license or for various operating permits just to do so. There may be a zoning law in your area that may severely limit exactly how many liquor licenses are sold in the state, county or municipality, forcing you to try to find a business that is selling its own liquor license. Some zoning laws may not allow alcohol to be sold at all, so it pays to know before you start.

Consumers like to make all of their shopping purchases in as few places as possible. Consumers love as much convenience as possible. Consider opening your liquor store in an area near a supermarket, laundromat, restaurant, fast-food business, auto mechanic, and other non-alcohol-related businesses.

Find a place that is sure to attract foot traffic and as strategically distant from your direct competitors as possible. Of course, you don't want to deal with your indirect competitors either, but not everyone drinks in a bar or at a restaurant. A lot of people like to get their alcohol to go, and you must find a site to serve those needs.

Choose the site location for your liquor store business wisely. Remember location, location, location. The location of your liquor store business will ultimately determine just how successful your business will be in the future.

## NAME YOUR BUSINESS

This is the first item on the list for several reasons. First, branding will be critical to your business. You have to stand out from the other shops near you; customers need to know why you are different and superior to your competition to give your liquor store a chance. So now you need a great name that stands out.

Here are some things to consider. Your name must be relevant in some way to who you are, your business, or your location. It needs to be connected to what you do. Your name should be short enough to be easily remembered. When you choose your name, it has to be unique, meaning not being used by any other company.

Google the name you have chosen and see if another business pops up. If it does not, you are in great shape. Checking your business name with the Patent and Trademark Office to ensure it is unique is another surefire method. Once you find the unique name you want, it is time to buy the domain for your business.

## Incorporating Your Business

Every business needs the proper licenses, permits, and other authorizations to conduct its normal course of business. When you choose a legal entity for your liquor store, there are two main factors to consider:

- What you want
- The type of business model you intend to build

Often, you can choose to file as a limited liability company (LLC), a general partnership, or a sole proprietorship. A sole proprietorship is the ideal business structure for someone starting a liquor store. However, most prefer the benefits of an LLC.

If you plan to eventually expand your liquor store to other locations or potentially online, then you definitely don't want to file as a sole proprietor. In this instance, you should definitely file as an LLC.

When you file as an LLC, you will be able to protect yourself from personal liability. This means that if anything goes wrong while operating your business, then only the money you invested in the company is at risk.

This isn't the case if you file as a sole proprietor or a general partnership. LLCs are simple and flexible to operate since you won't need a board of directors, shareholder meetings or other managerial formalities in order to run your business.

Here are all the legal business structures from which you can choose. It is best to get some advice from your CPA, accountant, or attorney.

## LEGAL BUSINESS STRUCTURE

When starting a business, there are five different business structures you can choose from:

- Sole Proprietor

- Partnership

- Corporation (Inc. or Ltd.)

- S Corporation

- Limited Liability Company (LLC)

## SOLE PROPRIETOR

This is not the safest structure for a liquor store. It is used for a business owned by a single person or a married couple. Under this structure, the owner is personally liable for all business debts and files in their personal income tax.

## PARTNERSHIP

If your business is owned and operated by multiple people, when it comes to structuring your business, you can choose one of two kinds of partnerships. These two kinds of partnerships are general partnerships and limited partnerships.

In a general partnership, the partners manage the business together and are responsible for each other debts. A limited partnership actually has both limited and general partners.

The general partners work as previously described, but the limited partners are only investors who don't actually have any control over the company and are not responsible for the debts in the same way.

## CORPORATION (INC. OR LTD.)

The corporate structure is complex and costs quite a bit more money than most other business structures. This is because a corporation is a completely independent legal entity. It is separate from its owners. It also requires you to comply with more regulations and requirements.

A corporation provides increased liability protection for the business owner or owners. A corporation's debt is not considered that of its owners. This lessens your personal risk.

It isn't a very common structure among liquor stores since there are shares of stocks involved.

Profits and taxes both are at the corporate level and distributed to shareholders. When you structure a business at this level, there are often lawyers involved.

## S CORPORATION

This is the most popular type of business entity people form to avoid double taxation. It is taxed similarly to a partnership entity. But an S Corp. needs to be approved to be classified as such, so it isn't very common among liquor stores.

The "S" corporation is going to be a more attractive option for small-business owners than a regular corporation. That's because an S corporation takes some great parts of what a corporation offers on a smaller, less expensive scale. It has some very appealing tax benefits as well as provides business owners with the liability protection of a corporation.

You have a couple of options for filing the paperwork required for your business. The first is to have a lawyer or accountant to file a legal business entity for you.

You can also do it yourself using online resources or by going to your local city office to fill out the necessary paperwork. You can go on websites like legalzoom.com and draw up the document for less money than what an attorney would charge you to do the same.

## LIMITED LIABILITY COMPANY (LLC)

This is the most common business structure among liquor stores. It offers benefits for small businesses since it reduces the risk of losing all your personal assets in case you are faced with a lawsuit. It provides a clear separation between business and personal assets. You can also elect to be taxed as a corporation, which saves you money come tax time.

If you are unsure which specific business structure you should choose, you can discuss it with an accountant. They will direct you to the best possible option for what your business goals are. You will find sample articles of incorporation at the end of the book. Just remember you should always get some sound legal advice when filing your corporation.

I filed my first LLC via Legalzoom.com as I didn't have the extra funds to hire an attorney. Thankfully, it worked out well for me.

## APPLY AND OBTAIN YOUR EMPLOYER IDENTIFICATION NUMBER FROM IRS

EIN or Employer Identification number is essentially a social security or tax identification number but for your business. The IRS and many other government agencies can identify your business using this unique nine-digit number.

Remember you will not need this number if you choose to be a sole proprietorship for your business.

It is simple to apply, either you can do it yourself or get your accountant to apply for you, but the process is simple, you fill out the form SS-4, which can be filed online, via Fax or via mail.

Here is a link to IRS website where you can download or fill out the form online.

https://www.irs.gov/businesses/small-businesses-self-employed/how-to-apply-for-an-ein

# SS-4

## Application for Employer Identification Number

Form SS-4
(Rev. January 2010)
Department of the Treasury
Internal Revenue Service

(For use by employers, corporations, partnerships, trusts, estates, churches, government agencies, Indian tribal entities, certain individuals, and others.)

► See separate instructions for each line.    ► Keep a copy for your records.

OMB No. 1545-0003

EIN

| 1 | Legal name of entity (or individual) for whom the EIN is being requested |
|---|---|

| 2 Trade name of business (if different from name on line 1) | 3 Executor, administrator, trustee, "care of" name |
|---|---|

| 4a Mailing address (room, apt., suite no. and street, or P.O. box) | 5a Street address (if different) (Do not enter a P.O. box.) |
|---|---|
| 4b City, state, and ZIP code (if foreign, see instructions) | 5b City, state, and ZIP code (if foreign, see instructions) |

| 6 | County and state where principal business is located |
|---|---|

| 7a Name of responsible party | 7b SSN, ITIN, or EIN |
|---|---|

8a Is this application for a limited liability company (LLC) (or a foreign equivalent)? . . . . . . . . ☐ Yes ☐ No    8b If 8a is "Yes," enter the number of LLC members . . . . . . ►

8c If 8a is "Yes," was the LLC organized in the United States? . . . . . . . . . . . . . . . . . . . ☐ Yes ☐ No

9a Type of entity (check only one box). Caution. If 8a is "Yes," see the instructions for the correct box to check.

☐ Sole proprietor (SSN) _____
☐ Partnership
☐ Corporation (enter form number to be filed) ► _____
☐ Personal service corporation
☐ Church or church-controlled organization
☐ Other nonprofit organization (specify) ► _____
☐ Other (specify) ►

☐ Estate (SSN of decedent)
☐ Plan administrator (TIN)
☐ Trust (TIN of grantor)
☐ National Guard ☐ State/local government
☐ Farmers' cooperative ☐ Federal government/military
☐ REMIC ☐ Indian tribal governments/enterprises
Group Exemption Number (GEN) if any ►

9b If a corporation, name the state or foreign country (if applicable) where incorporated | State | Foreign country

10 Reason for applying (check only one box)
☐ Started new business (specify type) ► _____
☐ Hired employees (Check the box and see line 13.)
☐ Compliance with IRS withholding regulations
☐ Other (specify) ►
☐ Banking purpose (specify purpose) ► _____
☐ Changed type of organization (specify new type) ► _____
☐ Purchased going business
☐ Created a trust (specify type) ► _____
☐ Created a pension plan (specify type) ► _____

| 11 Date business started or acquired (month, day, year). See instructions. | 12 Closing month of accounting year |
|---|---|

13 Highest number of employees expected in the next 12 months (enter -0- if none). If no employees expected, skip line 14.

14 If you expect your employment tax liability to be $1,000 or less in a full calendar year and want to file Form 944 annually instead of Forms 941 quarterly, check here. (Your employment tax liability generally will be $1,000 or less if you expect to pay $4,000 or less in total wages.) If you do not check this box, you must file Form 941 for every quarter. ☐

| Agricultural | Household | Other |
|---|---|---|

15 First date wages or annuities were paid (month, day, year). Note. If applicant is a withholding agent, enter date income will first be paid to nonresident alien (month, day, year) . . . . . . . . . . . . . . . . . . . . . . ►

16 Check one box that best describes the principal activity of your business. ☐ Health care & social assistance ☐ Wholesale-agent/broker
☐ Construction ☐ Rental & leasing ☐ Transportation & warehousing ☐ Accommodation & food service ☐ Wholesale-other ☐ Retail
☐ Real estate ☐ Manufacturing ☐ Finance & insurance ☐ Other (specify) ►

17 Indicate principal line of merchandise sold, specific construction work done, products produced, or services provided.

18 Has the applicant entity shown on line 1 ever applied for and received an EIN? ☐ Yes ☐ No
If "Yes," write previous EIN here ►

| Third Party Designee | Complete this section only if you want to authorize the named individual to receive the entity's EIN and answer questions about the completion of this form. | |
|---|---|---|
| | Designee's name | Designee's telephone number (include area code) |
| | Address and ZIP code | Designee's fax number (include area code) |

Under penalties of perjury, I declare that I have examined this application, and to the best of my knowledge and belief, it is true, correct, and complete.

Name and title (type or print clearly) ►

Applicant's telephone number (include area code)

Applicant's fax number (include area code)

68

This is an important step, but it can only be done after you have a fully executed article of incorporation approved by the state and an EIN assigned by the IRS.

Once you have these two documents, you should be able to open your first commercial bank account.

But remember to check and understand various types of commercial checking account fees. You want to find a bank that offers a free or almost free commercial checking account, because some larger banks can charge you hundreds of dollars each month, depending on how many transactions you do. Make sure to ask and shop around before you sign on the dotted line.

The next step would be to visit your local city and county business licensing office to find out which type of business and regulatory licenses you are required to have. It should take a few days to get your licenses and permits in place, and then you will be finally and officially in business.

## BUILD OUT/LAYOUT

You should look for storefronts, small buildings, and small properties for sale or long-term lease to purchase space for your liquor store. You should also consider buying an existing store, a small corner store, or a building, and then build out your liquor store business that way. Make every effort to buy a space that will serve your needs and require little renovation or repair work, which would just be added expenses.

Display liquor, beer, and wine products you know are good sellers, with full display and promotional placards. Navigating a liquor store and finding a specific item can be confusing for new customers in unfamiliar spaces, so do everything you can to make the experience as convenient as possible.

**(Source: Progressive Grocer)**

You should have a dedicated section for all "hard liquors." Next to them, you should have an area dedicated to cocktail mixers and all other cocktail-mixing accessories. Next, you need an area for all your wine, but remember to display by price point, not by name. Most expensive wines should be all the way to the top, and similarly, cheaper ones at the bottom.

The other end of your store should have a 5-7-door cooler where you display all your imported and domestic beer. Remember to follow the price flow here, too. Next to the beer cooler, have a few reach-in coolers for chilled wines, various juices and water.

Next, dedicate a section to high-quality snacks, such as peanuts, cookies, and munchies. Keep in mind that these snacks should complement your beer, wine and liquor.

Behind the checkout counter, you will need racks to display your cigars, cigarettes and tobacco. Try to carry a good variety of cigars. Sometimes, you will find that people will visit your store based on how big your cigar selection is.

Lastly, set up a display of all your hookahs and their accessories around the front windows.

Here is a well-researched fact that should encourage you to do your own research to learn more about your customer demographic. Over 93% of consumers who buy liquor in liquor stores also buy beer. Consumers who visit liquor stores only to buy beer, however, account for only about 37% of visits, according to research.[8] So, it is your job to research which liquor, wines and spirits products would most likely appeal to beer drinkers and how to convert such beer drinkers to buy more non-beer alcohol products. How your store layout displays advertisements and products in your liquor store business can help immensely with your liquor conversion strategy with beer drinkers.

Also, remember to use creative lighting displays to showcase the inventory products you want to sell. Flat, uniform lighting throughout your store will be visually boring to consumers. Hang signs that display what kind of alcohol can be found in each aisle. Take every step to make your liquor store as visually inviting to consumers as possible.

Work with an industry consultant or seek advice from a liquor store owner on possible store layouts. You should also visit a few liquor stores yourself, maybe even your direct competitors, just to see how they lay out their businesses decoratively and promotionally.

8 "Liquor Stores." Progressive Grocer, vol. 96, no. 8, Aug. 2017, pp. 18-23.

# MERCHANDISING, EQUIPMENT & VENDOR SELECTION

Merchandising is essentially what you carry in your store to sell to your customer base. A common misconception about liquor stores is that is a liquor store only carry liquor, beer, and wine. But that is not true. A typical liquor store carries a wide variety of products, as do most convenience stores and gas stations. But the law regarding what you can carry in your liquor store may vary widely by city and state. For example, in Alabama, the law says you cannot carry any milk or deli food in a liquor store. But you are okay to carry candy, cookies, chips, soft drinks, water, cigarettes, tobacco, and beauty-related products.

Your goal is to make your liquor store as much of a neighborhood convenience store as possible, so customers can do one-stop shopping. Most liquor stores have the following categories of sales.

| ITEMS | PERCENTAGE OF SALES |
|---|---|
| Liquor, Beer & Wine Sales | 40% |
| Cigarette & Tobacco Sales | 25% |
| Soda & N/A Drink Sales | 15% |
| Candy, Chips, Snacks Sales | 10% |
| Hookahs & Other Sales | 10% |
| **TOTAL** | **100%** |

The liquor industry business practice of promoting and displaying your most expensive, best-selling, and customer-preferred liquor products as prominently as possible. Merchandising is also a form of subtle psychological warfare. Trying to get people to buy something new, beyond their preferred alcoholic beverage choice, can be very difficult. People want what they want and are sometimes resistant to change.

Also, while it is imperative that you do everything you can to encourage and retain loyal customers, you will always have new customers walk in the front door of your liquor store business who don't know the first thing about alcohol or what they want.

Merchandising is a way of selling ideas, too, like the idea that drinking a particular brand of liquor makes a person hip, cool, or in the know. People in the digital age research and study alcoholic products online and know what they want. A lot of people know nothing about alcohol and are very susceptible to sleek advertising as well.

There is another reason you will want to devote as much time and energy as possible to best-merchandising practices. It's called R.O.I., or return on investment. Depending on your start-up investing capital, filling your initial start-up inventory could cost anywhere between $50,000 $100,000, and even a *lot* more than that.

You are going to pay a lot of money to stock your inventory and shelves with Absolut vodka, Johnnie Walker whiskey, and many other well-known, name-brand alcoholic drinks.

**(Sources: Justin Holman)**

Another thing you must learn about and take into account is the down-level moving only alcohol industry distribution wholesale system. In the United States, as per regulations, Alcohol can only be sold by wineries and producers to wholesale distributors, then to retailers like you, the private businessperson and then you sell it to consumers. You cannot skip a tier in the system and buy from wineries or producers; this system only goes downward. You can only buy your inventory from a licensed distributor in your state. There may be a few licensed distributors in your state. There also might be only one licensed distributor in your whole state, which will take negotiation off the table.

They will sell products at wholesale prices, and you won't be able to shop around for the best price if there is only one distributor.[9] Your best bet may be to buy products by bulk volume that you know will sell well. Wholesale distributors may also offer nice discounts for such purchases.

Excess inventory and bottles sitting on your shelf won't help you turn a profit, so you should do everything that you can to move your product out the door and make a profit. This might be another reason for you to check out your direct competition and see how they merchandise. Or take the counsel of an industry consultant or another liquor store owner who is not in direct competition with you.

9 Holman, Justin. *"The 3 Lessons I Learned After Accidentally Buying a Liquor Store."* February 18, 2014. http://www.justinholman.com/2014/02/18/the-3-lessons-i-learned-when-i-accidentally-bought-a-liquor-store/

When opening a liquor store, there are so many things you need to make it work. Having the right reach-in and walk-in coolers and other shelvings is essential to your new liquor store's success.

Before buying anything, you'll want to decide whether you plan to buy the equipment upfront or prefer a lease option. The choice to lease or buy will have a significant impact on the budget.

Leasing equipment can free up cash flow, but reading the fine print is essential. You don't want to end up paying significantly more in the long run. I personally do not prefer the leasing option, but I wanted to mention it so you know it is an option.

Once you've decided on whether to buy or lease, or maybe a bit of both, you can now start to choose your vendors. Begin the search for a vendor the simplest way: a Google search for convenience store equipment vendors. This will enable you to look at both local and national vendors that will get you started on the right foot.

Another great option is to take advantage of going-out-of-business sales. Opening a business can be difficult, so unfortunately, this is a viable way to obtain the equipment you need.

When a business closes, it often tries to sell its equipment to get back as much money as possible before it has to close its doors. So, if you know of any restaurants or other food service providers near you that are closing, try tracking down the owner and see if they would be interested in selling any of their equipment. If they are, you can often purchase the equipment they have at significantly discounted prices.

Using social media and digital yard sales is another option. This has really become a very popular option in today's age. Social media platforms like Facebook and Twitter now offer online marketplaces where you can sell any items, both household and commercial items, you no longer want. There are also online platforms dedicated to this type of selling; the popular app  letgo.com is one.

Finally, there are equipment auctions. This is a great source for buying used equipment. There are companies that hold auctions all across the country for all kinds of restaurant equipment.

They are heavily discounted. You could luck out and purchase several pieces of much-needed equipment this way. This is an amazing option if you can find one within driving distance. Even if you have to drive a bit, it is worth taking a ride to see what discounts are available.

Here are some places you can look for good used coolers and other equipment online. Please understand that I am not an affiliate for any of these companies, so do your research and compare prices before buying.

http://www.ebay.com/bhp/used-restaurant-equipment

https://www.acitydiscount.com/

http://kescoflorida.com/

https://www.webstaurantstore.com/restaurant-equipment.html

http://www.jeansrestaurantsupply.com/restaurant-equipment/used-restaurant-equipment.html

In addition, you can also search your local newspaper, Craigslist and local in-town equipment dealers.

## VENDOR SELECTION

I am sure this question occurred to you at least once while reading this book. You must have wondered where to buy your supplies from. Well, this is the easy part. Every city has a handful of beer, liquor, and wine distributors. You can find them in the yellow pages or by a simple Google search. The best part is that there is no price negotiation with these vendors in most cases.

You are wondering why I am saying that it is a good thing, right? Well, here is why. Say Budweiser is charging you $4.50 for each six-pack of beer, rest assured, they are charging the same price to Wal-Mart, Target, and your next-door competitors. So, no one has any extra advantage over you because you are the small guy and they own over 100 locations.

To me, that is a huge plus. Similarly, most wine and liquor distributors follow the same guidelines. But I will add that, at times, they do offer a volume discount to all retailers. For example, a wine vendor may offer you $4 off each case if you buy 50 or more cases in a month; that is a promotional price for every retailer, but it is a volume discount. In my opinion, if you have the extra cash, go ahead and buy this way. You will sell for the same price but keep the extra $ 4 per case in your pocket.

To find suppliers for other merchandise, you can look for local grocery supply companies; again, a simple Google search can reveal a few names in your area. Alternatively, you can walk into a gas station or convenience store in your area and ask the manager where they buy their groceries, and find a few local grocery stores that way.

If you are selling cigarettes and tobacco in your store, you can either buy all your tobacco and cigarettes from the grocery company or you can simply go to your local Sam's Club or Costco and buy from them. These two big wholesalers tend to beat almost every other wholesaler's price. Don't forget to contact the three major tobacco companies to open a rebate account with each so you can get "Buy Down" funds.

This fund will allow you to sell cigarettes and tobacco cheaper and let you compete with many big retailers. Ask your grocery or Sam's Club associate for the local contact numbers for all three tobacco representatives.

Lastly, for your hookah supplier, look on Alibaba.com, where you will find a wide variety of hookahs at a very reasonable price. But for their accessories and tobacco, you should find local suppliers.

Here are a few websites that you can look and to see who offers the best deals.

https://www.hookahwholesalers.com/

https://www.southsmoke.com/

https://www.thehookah.com/pages/hookah-wholesale

# PRICING & POS

How much income do you think you will be able to generate in a week, month, or even annually with your liquor store business? How much revenue, or profits used to pay expenses, do you think you will have to pay on a monthly basis? What do you believe will be your profit margins? How much did you pay for your inventory, and how much product do you need to sell each week, month, half-year, and year to break even and turn a profit? What are the market and usual retail prices to sell your products? What products sell fast and sluggishly?

You should take all of these factors into account as you set your pricing list. Also, your Alcoholic Beverage Control board will have a pricing guide for all alcoholic beverages sold in your state that you should refer to as well.

Consider it a control list to guide you as you calculate your own prices. You won't be able to charge just any price that you want for your inventory product. So, you should make precise, studious calculations to determine what to charge legally for your product, without running afoul of regulations. At the same time, while doing all of that, you also want to turn a profit.

Here is a typical profit margin for all products carried in a liquor store.

| CATEGORY/ITEMS | PROFIT MARGIN |
|:---:|:---:|
| Liquor | 40-45% |
| Beer | 17%-23% |
| Wine | 25%-35% |
| Cigarette | 15%-19% |
| Tobacco | 20%-25% |

| | |
|---|---|
| Soda & Other Drinks | 30%-35% |
| Snacks, Chips, and Cookies | 35%-40% |
| Candy & Gum | 35%-45% |
| Health & Beauty Products | 45%-50% |
| Hookah & Accessories | 45%-50% |
| All Other items | 35%-50% |

You need to calculate how much inventory you need to sell and at what prices to carefully figure out your profit. You may need to buy a lot of inventory in bulk, per distributor mandates, so you can offer your customers a "buy one, get one half-price" deal. However, in whatever manner that you decide to price your inventory products, it must be in a way that benefits your inventory turnover rate, budget, accounting, revenue margins, and need for profit margins.

Making such calculations and pricing all of your inventory will take long hours of work and meticulous bookkeeping. Be prepared for that. Also, when it is time for sales or to discount certain products to move lingering products off the shelves, you will have to make adjusted calculations for that as well. Owning a liquor store business will involve extremely long hours doing things like this, bean-counting, paper-pushing and crunching the numbers. Your pricing practices should also be the result of your studious bookkeeping. As you should realize by now, no actions related to the operations of a liquor store business should be random or done without studied forethought.

## UNDERSTANDING PENNY PROFIT, PROFIT MARGIN, AND MARKUP

In business, these are the three most common terms we hear every day, but what do they all mean, and how they are different from each other, is a question many of you have.

Okay, let's break them down and see what they are:

Penny profit is essentially the actual cash profit you make by selling any items in your store. For example, say you just sold a 20-oz bottle. Coke for $1.75, what is the penny profit from that sale? To find the answer, we first need to know how much you paid for that bottle of Coke.

Looking at your invoice from Coke, you paid $1.00 for that bottle of Coke and sold it for $1.75. So, your penny profit is $1.75 -$ 1.00 = 75 cents. Penny profit is the difference between the selling price and- actual costs.

## PROFIT MARGIN

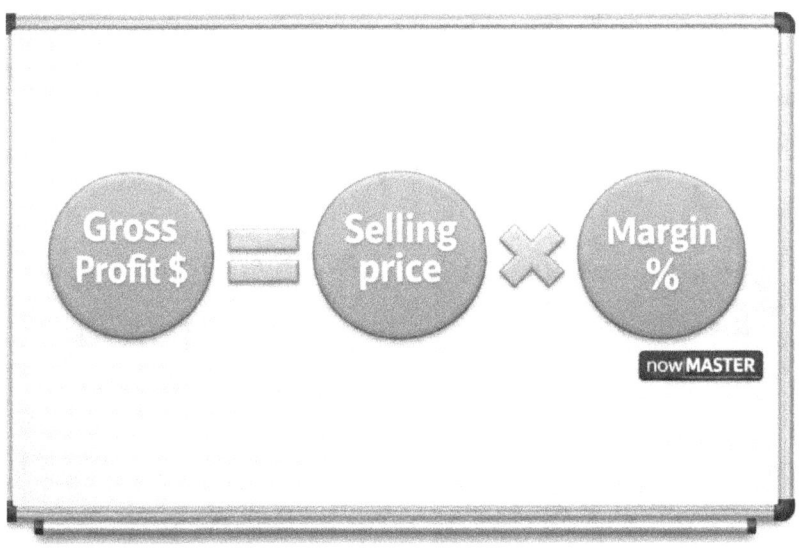

Profit margin is the term most widely used and understood in business, as it shows whether we are making enough profit from selling products and services.

Profit margin is essentially the percentage of profit you make or earn when you sell a product. Confusing? Let's take a look at the same example of that bottle of Coke we just used earlier.

We already know the penny profit from that sale was 75 cents. Now, the profit margin is calculated a little differently; to find the exact margin, we will have to take the penny profit and divide it by the selling price. So, it will be $ 1.75- $ 1.00 = 0.75; then we divide that penny profit by the selling price: 0.75/$1.75 = 43% profit margin.

## MARKUP

The markup, on the other hand, is somewhat similar to profit margin, but instead of dividing the penny profit by the selling price, you would have to divide the penny profit by the actual cost. Let's take a look at the same example once again.

Remember our penny profit from that bottle of Coke? It was 75 cents; now we just need to divide that by the actual cost, which was $1.00, right? Let's do this:

$0.75/\$1.00 = 75\%$ Markup for that same bottle of Coke.

# POS (POINT OF SALES SYSTEM)

While you will be responsible for much of the physical accounting of your inventory products, we also live in an era where you can make the most of digital accounting software and technology to track sales transactions much faster and infinitely more accurately. POS (point of sale) computer hardware, like cash registers and scanning technology, as well as software, are what modern retail businesses use to conduct transactions and sales on the spot, record them, and save this information for payment and accounting purposes later.

POS, in business terms, refers to the location where a consumer pays a merchant for a service or product using a digital device. In this sense, which would mean a consumer walks into your liquor store, hands you a bottle of liquor, pays for it with cash, a debit card, or a credit card at the cash register, and you, as the proprietor, complete the sale and transaction.

Look at it another way. If you have ever gone to the supermarket, put your groceries on the conveyor belt in front of the cashier as you wait for them to be scanned, then you have used a POS transaction system many times before. The prices, sales, and discount values of every bottle and can in your inventory can be programmed into a POS system and then automatically recalled during the sale transaction using the POS technology, the physical cash register, and the scanner.

You should invest in POS-compatible cash registers and scanners, as well as the accompanying licensed POS software, which may need to be frequently updated. You won't actually own the POS software system; you will actually just be purchasing a license to use it for your business purposes. People who use Apple technology products, like an iPad, are basically purchasing a license to use them if they bother to read the fine print. POS systems record all sales transactions instantly and support transaction accounting, whether by cash, credit card, or debit.

POS technology should be considered a valuable aid in keeping your accounting and bookkeeping as accurate as possible. Before the advent of POS technology and software, every product needed an identifying sales tag that was then rung up on pre-computerized cash registers. Each transaction then had to be tracked and verified by hand. Such information is stored on product barcodes or data-instilled stickers. POS technology and software are fast, efficient and extremely accurate. It also significantly reduces human error and the costly, time-consuming mistakes that can result from it. You can instantly retrieve all data related to a transaction, instead of searching through file folders of records.

Look at it another way. As the owner of a liquor store business, you will have an inventory that will include hundreds, if not *thousands*, of branded products. Each product in your inventory will have its own unique price point or suggested retailer's selling price. You will undoubtedly run promotional or cost-cutting sales on particular products. You can account for each price yourself at checkout with a pencil, paper, and calculator, like it is 1984, or you can let your POS technology systems and software handle most of the hard accounting work for you.

POS technology and software are simply a quicker, more accurate way to automatically generate accounting records for all your sales transactions. Your liquor store business is a retail business, just like any restaurant or supermarket. Convenience and efficiency for yourself and your customers should be paramount, so you should definitely invest in POS technology and software. It will definitely make your transition into a liquor store business owner much smoother. As previously mentioned, such systems will be invaluable to your accounting and bookkeeping activities.

Without an efficient and reliable point-of-sale system, your business can be slowed down by payment processing lags, poor inventory management, and untimely service and repairs. But if your POS is cloud-based, you won't have to worry about tracking your data or inventory, since the system will handle it for you. Luckily, cloud-based POS systems are not only lightning-fast but also reliable.

But these systems are so much more than bundles of software and hardware. With one ergonomic terminal, you can also track your business's analytics and profits, manage inventory, and oversee email marketing to bring in new customers.

You may need all items on this liquor store equipment list, or just a few. There is no absolute recipe for success when opening a liquor store. To understand what will work for you, be aware of the demographic you are serving and their needs and wants. Do not buy equipment you do not need or that you are unsure how to use.

When buying new equipment, always be aware of the wide-eyed syndrome. Let's face it. some things just look cool, and we want them, but this is not the place for impulse buying. That money would be better spent on things you really need. Buying things that appear fancy and high-tech will lead you nowhere.

Here is a link to a website where you can see all the top brand POS systems for a reasonable price for your liquor store. Don't worry, most of these POS systems can be customized to exactly what you want in a POS.

https://www.softwareadvice.com/retail/liquor-store-software-comparison/

# GRAND OPENING

The grand opening of your liquor store business will be your announcement to the neighborhood that you are now open for business and ready to serve all of their alcohol-related needs. However, you shouldn't just open your liquor store business suddenly or out of the blue in a marketing vacuum.

Your customer base, the people, and workers in the local neighborhood, offices, businesses and organizations in your neighborhood, should know that you are going to open your liquor store business doors weeks, if not months, before you actually open its doors.

You should announce your liquor store's opening on social media and make as many local connections as you can in the neighborhood where you plan to operate. You can also pay for signs and street ads to promote your grand opening.

You may try to become the local supplier for any local restaurants, clubs, and eateries in the area. Especially if you have done your research and know that you are opening your store with some healthy strategic distance away from your direct competitors. Calculate how much you can charge local restaurants, diners, and eateries that will undercut your direct competition and still ensure you a profit.

Make such inroad connections early in your business endeavor, like after you acquire your liquor license and before the grand opening. Make strategic use of this time to develop these relationships with local businesses and finesse ways to promote your grand opening as well.

Check out any colleges, art galleries, organizations and any place of business that will allow you to hold wine tasting events, barring any zoning law restrictions. Make such connections to promote contests or events at your grand opening, where you will give out T-shirts, discounts, or limited-edition product as prizes. You could pay for a local performing group to perform in front of your grand opening, but that will be an extra expense, and you may need a permit for such. You could also hire or make arrangements with a food truck business to be parked outside your liquor store's grand opening to offer food to your customers, but such an arrangement may require a permit as well.

Sponsor a local, adult-age sporting event. Sponsor a local talent show, fashion show or neighborhood association picnic or public event. You have to find ways to get your liquor store's name out there and ensure your local demographic knows you are opening. You can pay for TV commercials and radio advertisements, but we live in the digital age now. The promotional reach of your liquor store business will extend much further online and on social media.

Find out every social media site on the internet that is connected to or associated with the neighborhood in which your liquor store business operates. Make sure the inhabitants of your neighborhood know your business exists well before your grand opening.

# BOOKKEEPING AND ACCOUNTING

Many businesspeople who open a liquor store fail within the first year of operations because they dream of how easy it will be to open and run one. A liquor store is supposed to be a recession-proof business endeavor, right? Well, not so fast. Nothing that is worthwhile in life, like running a business, is ever easy.

Running a business like this involves hard work and extreme, meticulous attention to detail. That means long hours in the office, going over the numbers. Then, going over the numbers again. Then, go over the numbers again. Then, going over the numbers again. If your bookkeeping numbers are off, even a little, it can affect your profit margin, your taxes, your ability to expand or pay for new inventory, and your ability to portray your liquor store business positively in your updated business plans.

This is where your bookkeeping and accounting skills, or the people you hire to handle such tasks, will come into play.

Let's start by differentiating between bookkeeping and accounting. Bookkeeping is the art of minutely recording every sales and purchase transaction connected to your liquor store business. All the money you make from selling your inventory must be recorded in your books or official record of transactions.

Any money you pay for repairs must be recorded in your books. All of the money you spend on payroll, for revenue, and for inventory turnover must be recorded in your books. Accounting is the business-related study of your business's bookkeeping records for tax purposes, business plan implementation, liquor license reapplications, and all similar purposes. A bookkeeper officially records your business records, and an accountant makes sense of them for any other endeavor that is related to your bookkeeping.

You may need to act as your own bookkeeper and accountant, or hire professionals to help you. Since you are the owner of your liquor store business, you should be intimately familiar with your business's bookkeeping records and accounting, whether you hire professionals to officially do them or not.

You have to pay for utilities and rent. If you plan to hire employees, you will have to pay for payroll. Liquor licenses expire, and you must reapply for them annually or every three years, depending on where you live. You have to turn over, or replenish your exhausted inventory supplies of alcohol with reorders, regularly. You may have to pay for shop repairs or pay for occasional shrinkage.

Liquor liability insurance premiums and any other insurance products that you will need to pay for your liquor store business won't pay for themselves. The point is that you will be liable for many expenses or revenue payments before you hopefully see any profits.

Your accounting and bookkeeping must be unerringly accurate to the penny if you have any hope of being successful as a liquor store business owner. Every bottle in your inventory that leaves your business through the front door with a customer is a potential source of profit. You have to keep track of and account for each and every product in your inventory.

Buying a liquor license means that you have the proprietary permission to sell alcoholic beverages, under laws and regulations as defined by your state, city and local municipality, to the general public. Every sale you make has to be recorded and accounted for, for tax purposes, profit realization purposes, or to implement in your updated business plans from time to time.

Every bottle of merchandise that comes in and out of your front door, as per sales, must be documented and accounted for in your records accurately every time. This can't be stated enough. Your liquor store business bookkeeping must always be in order. Additionally, for tax purposes, business plan purposes, liquor license reacquisition purposes, business loan purposes and a host of other reasons, your books may be requested for accounting study and reference.

You can make use of the latest in accounting software to help you keep accurate accounting books. Also, as previously discussed. POS technology and software programs will help you keep accurate records of every transaction at your liquor store. You can also hire a private accountant to help with all of your number crunching, but that will also be another added expense on top of your many business expenses.

Most importantly, you need to know how well you are doing with ROI (return on investment) on your inventory purchases. You need to know how much money you are making or losing based on these variables. If you do not endeavor to keep track of all your transactions and business purposes with the accounting and bookkeeping acumen of an auditing IRS agent, then you will be just wasting your time and even more money trying to run a liquor store business.

# MARKETING & PROMOTION

As I have mentioned numerous times before, we live in the digital age. Almost half of the planet is connected to the internet and uses social media platforms like Facebook, Instagram, Twitter, and Reddit. That is more than three billion people. While you may not be able to connect to three billion people (try your best, however), there is no reason why you can't take every initiative to make the most of social media to effectively market your liquor store business.

Learn about every social media website connected to the neighborhood from which you run and operate your liquor store business. Create a business e-newsletter to remind people of your store's location, sales, discounts, and events. It will be an extra added expense, but it may be very worth it for you to hire a graphic designer or web designer to create and main a website for your liquor store business. Unless you are dealing with a small business demographic, flyers, placards, street signs and billboards will only get you so far in the digital age. Make customer connections online whenever possible. In the digital age, most people, especially millennials aged 18 to 34, are more likely to pay attention to an ad on their mobile devices than to a street billboard or flyer.

Another reason to market online is that people are much savvier about liquor, wine, and beer than ever before. People research their favorite alcoholic beverages and write online blogs about them. Try to cater to that audience. I mentioned before that you could reach out to businesses and art galleries to hold wine, cheese, and hors d'oeuvres tastings. You can do the same thing in your liquor store business. Offer small, free food samples alongside liquor product samples to encourage sales. Remember, after all, it takes money to make money.

A great way to market your liquor store business is to have regular contests. Give away products, t-shirts, hats, and other small prizes that show a genuine effort to reach your customer base.

Hire a professional bartender to come in regularly and hold free mixology classes. Invite as many of your customers as possible, and advertise these classes in your online e-newsletter. Make sure the bartender uses liquor products in the mixology class that are readily available in your store. This way, anyone who attends the classes and wants to recreate the drinks will have the buy the products from you.

This would be a great way to market your liquor store business and the products that you want to sell. According to liquor industry market research, the number one selling vodka product in the year 2016 was Smirnoff vodka.[10] Of course, as a businessperson, you must endeavor to learn exactly what your customer demographic wants to drink and serve their need. You should also make the most of market research, as that will serve your need to succeed and profit.

10 Global vodka market: leading brands 2016, based on sales volume
https://www.statista.com/statistics/259727/leading-vodka-brands-worldwide-based-on-sales-volume/

## The leading selling vodka brands worldwide in 2016, based on sales volume (in million 9-liter cases)

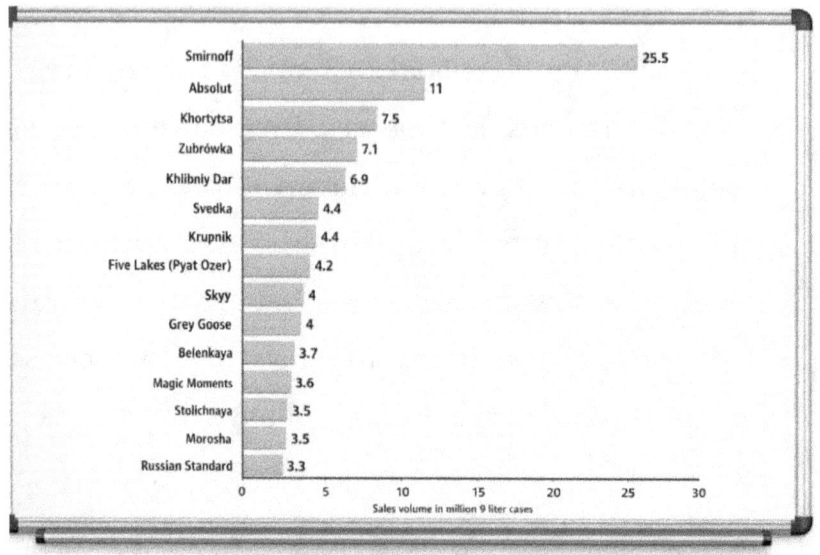

**(Source: Statista)**

You can also take an old-world approach and mail flyers advertising the opening of your liquor store. Although you should be prepared to mail hundreds, if not thousands, of such advertising postcards or letters to market your business. You may be able to buy customer addresses from your wholesale distributor or other local businesses in the area. You should also encourage people online, on your website, and on social media to provide their basic address and contact information in exchange for promotional updates.

These basic ideas and tips should really act as a template for your own marketing plans. Be creative. Think about marketing your liquor store business in a way that makes the most of the knowledge you have about the market, your customer demographic, your neighborhood base of operations and your inventory products.

# HOW TO GROW YOUR NEW BUSINESS

As I have previously explained, some liquor industry analysts have stated that the liquor store business is among the least profitable businesses one can start. On the other hand, the liquor industry in the United States of America is also worth tens of billions of dollars annually, so that fact must be considered as well. A lot of small businesses fail within the first few years of operation, but by those numbers, someone in the liquor business must be succeeding as well.

When you take into consideration the ardent and strictly enforced liquor industry regulations, buying inventory from a handful or even one distributor, and the tight profit margins to be gained when you factor in revenue payments, you may want to use the success of your first liquor store business to expand into multiple franchise stores. Remember, in mid-sized and large cities, multiple liquor store businesses are needed to meet demand. There is never just one liquor store business in a metropolitan neighborhood. Usually, in such circumstances, one businessperson has expanded from a single store to several.

Any eventual expansion plans for your liquor store business will be predicated on the success of your first store. So, you should brainstorm ways to grow your liquor store business, increase profits organically, and do so in a way that serves everyone in your neighborhood. You should consider selling other products that people will come to your liquor store business to buy. You will sell an additional product, and there will always be the potential to convert to liquor sales.

Start selling lottery tickets in your liquor store business. You will be guaranteed to bring in extra foot traffic to your store if you sell lottery tickets, and it will be more likely than not that you will experience a lot of liquor conversion sales from lottery ticket buyers. The lottery business is a multi-billion-dollar business on an annual basis. There are lottery ticket consumers who buy lottery tickets daily, weekly, monthly and annually on a habitual basis.

According to industry research, almost 9.7 billion dollars' worth of lottery tickets were sold in the year 2016. In that same year, over 6 billion dollars' worth of lottery tickets were sold in California and Florida. In that same time period, well over $ 5 billion in lottery tickets were sold in both Massachusetts and Texas.

Yes, you are in the liquor store business, but even supermarkets sell a variety of products, not just one. You can even sell cigarettes as well to entice extra foot traffic, just as long as the sin taxes of your state, or taxation for vice-enabling products like alcohol or cigarettes, are not too high for your bottom line.

Consider selling soft drinks and juices as well, since many people make their own mixed drinks at home. This will also help your sales if you opt to have a bartender come in to teach complimentary in-store mixology classes from time to time.

**Sales of lotteries in the United States in 2016, state to state (in billion U.S. dollars)**

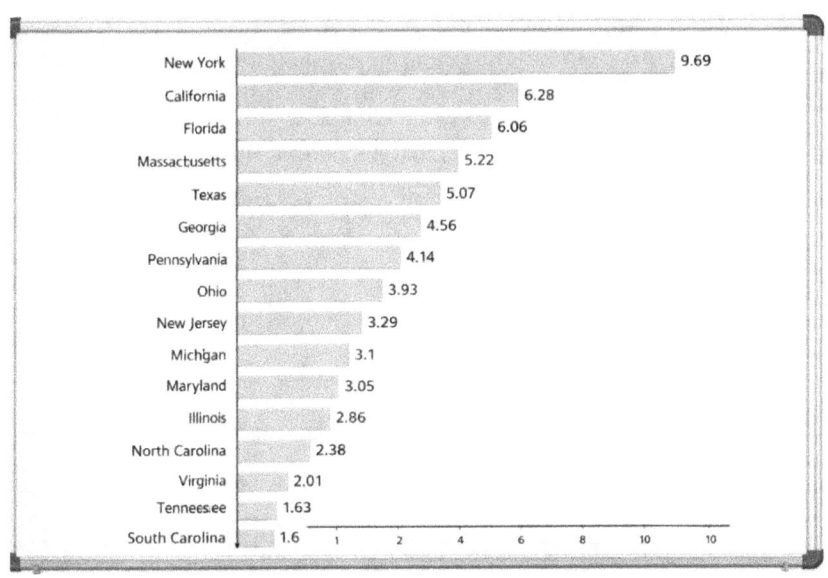

| | |
|---|---|
| New York | 9.69 |
| California | 6.28 |
| Florida | 6.06 |
| Massachusetts | 5.22 |
| Texas | 5.07 |
| Georgia | 4.56 |
| Pennsylvania | 4.14 |
| Ohio | 3.93 |
| New Jersey | 3.29 |
| Michigan | 3.1 |
| Maryland | 3.05 |
| Illinois | 2.86 |
| North Carolina | 2.38 |
| Virginia | 2.01 |
| Tenneesee | 1.63 |
| South Carolina | 1.6 |

**(Source: Statista)**

Consider selling soft drinks and juices as well, since many people make their own mixed drinks at home. This will also help your sales if you opt to have a bartender come in to teach complimentary in-store mixology classes from time to time.

Also, remember that consumers love the convenience and want to do all of their shopping in as few places as possible. You don't have to convert your liquor store business into a mini-supermarket, but offering complementary products, like lottery tickets, soft drinks, gum, and cigarettes, can go a long way towards creating conversion sales towards liquor.

Most people don't just walk into a liquor store to buy gum, a lottery ticket, or a can of soda, then leave. Offer your customer demographic a few more product options, and extra conversion sales are sure to follow.

Keep meticulous track of sales after a few months and adjust your bookkeeping and accounting, as necessary. Adjust your business plan, as necessary. If you can show that your new product additions have increased profits, and/or instigated numerous consumer conversion sales, then such numbers will reflect positively on your bookkeeping and adjusted business plan.

That will, in turn, reflect positively when you submit your revised and updated business plan to potential investors, banks, and business loan finance lenders. Your best option for growth or opening expansion locations is a business loan or a significant investment from a business partner.

If you can open one liquor store business, you can open another one. All it takes is a strategy, using a business-centric eye to discern how the market can work for you, brainstorming conversion-focused sales strategies, and understanding your customer base.

11 Sales of lotteries in the U.S. 2016, by state. https://www.statista.com/statistics/388238/sales-of-lotteries-by-state-us/

# CONCLUSION

Every neighborhood needs and requires business people dedicated to buttressing the economy of the neighborhood. Like the neighborhood supermarket. The neighborhood deli. The neighborhood laundromat. The neighborhood auto shop. The neighborhood dental office.

The neighborhood liquor store is part of basic neighborhood business infrastructure. It's an avenue of reliable business and a solid opportunity. As previously mentioned, most neighborhoods have multiple liquor store businesses operating within their boundaries.

Throughout this book, I have given you tips, ideas, and advice on how to start and manage your own liquor store business. You will need legal counsel. You will need to scout out potential locations to start your liquor store business. You will need to inquire about start-up financing. You will need to learn about your inventory, hopefully with the input of a liquor industry consultant or the advice of another liquor store business owner who won't be in direct competition with you. You will have to fill out more paperwork and apply for more operational licenses than you may be comfortable with. Most of all, you will need money, lots of money, as it takes a lot of start-up capital to open a liquor store business.

Most of all, however, opening a liquor store business will require drive and a willingness to spend long hours at the offices going over bookkeeping and accounting. You won't be able to be an absentee boss when it comes to owning and operating a liquor store business. Even if you hire employees to aid you in operating your liquor store business, or businesses, it should only be for oversight purposes.

The success of your liquor store business will depend entirely on you and what you alone as the owner are willing to do to see it prosper. You can't and shouldn't cede such authority to an employee, bookkeeper, or accountant. Your employees shouldn't know more about your business operations than you. When you start your liquor store business, you will undoubtedly have hundreds, if not thousands, of inventory product on your shelves. You must be intimately knowledgeable, at all times, about the status of every bottle in your inventory and even cent generated in sales.

If you hire employees, their part-time or full-time status as workers will only involve a finite number of working hours each week. As the owner of a liquor store business, you will be working 24-hours a day and seven days a week to stay on top of the operations of your business. You have to always be involved, and you have to stay continually abreast of what going on with your business.

If not, you are just wasting time and money. Remember, only about 37% of businesses ever succeed, profit and stay in business after four years of operation. You can be part of the 37% that succeed. You *should* be part of that 37% that succeeds in business.

It's up to and only you. You will have to sacrifice a lot of free time and be good with mathematics. Or take some refresher courses in mathematics if necessary. No one should know your bookkeeping and accounting numbers better than you after all. It's your business about which we are talking.

Yes, people will always need to drink alcohol. People will always need to drink alcohol during the good times and especially the bad times. Owning a liquor store business may be the closest thing to owning a recession-proof business endeavor.

You will always need to run your liquor store business. During the good times and especially during any bad times. You can only dream of expansion if you are successful with the first one. It takes dedication, drive, and discipline to run a liquor store business.

There is a famous quote that says there is no real secret checklist or formula for success in business. Fortune favors the knowledgeably prepared. Long work hours, being prepared for anything and learning the reasons for failure, not folding because of it, will help you to go a long way in business.

You are going to open a liquor store business.

You can do it. You have the drive to do it. You are reading this book for a reason.

If it isn't you, it will be someone else.

# LAST WORDS

In this book, I have outlined the steps to successfully opening a liquor store. After reading this book, if you decide to open such a store, it is time to develop a solid, precise business plan, as I discussed at the beginning.

No, I am not asking you to write a 50-page business plan, but a plan that outlines where you will get the funding, what you want in your liquor store, and what area of the city you want this business to be in, and in what time you want to accomplish this goal. A plan where you figure out in which direction you will take your business.

Remember, you only get one chance to make a great first impression, so when planning, make sure you add some "wow" factors. This way, you will make a great first impression. To make such an impression, you don't need to spend extra money; you just need to be creative and figure out what makes customers go "wow."

Keep your focus on the quality and marketing side of your business, and you will see success sooner rather than later.

Hopefully, this book gives you a good general overview of how to start a trendy liquor store. Now get out there and start figuring out how you can make this dream a reality. And be successful. Remember, we only live once, so why not try to be the best you can be and see where that may take you?

I wanted to thank you for buying my book; I am not a professional writer or author, but rather someone who has always had a passion for starting various c-store businesses. In this book, I wanted to share my knowledge with you, as I know many people share the same passion and drive as I do. This book is dedicated to YOU, my readers.

Despite my best efforts to make this book error-free, if you find any mistakes, please forgive me.

Just remember, my writing skills may not be the best, but the knowledge I share here is pure and honest.

If you thought I added value and shared information you can use, please take a minute to post a review on the site where you bought this book. I read every review I get, and if you leave your contact information, I will personally email you to say "Thanks." This will mean the world to me. Thank you so much!!

Lastly, I wanted to thank my wife, Dawn, and my daughter, Jessica, for all their help and support throughout this book; without them, this book would not have been possible.

Once again, thank you from the bottom of my heart for reading this book. I wish you all the best of luck, great success and happiness in life.

www.ingramcontent.com/pod-product-compliance
Lightning Source LLC
Chambersburg PA
CBHW071320220526
45468CB00001B/436